The Beginner's Guide to Cryptocurrencies: What the New Rich Investor Teach Their Followers About Virtual Money

Five Parameters to Analyze, How to Create Your Asset and Choose the Best Currencies

By
Mike Armstrong

advice. The content within this Story has been derived from various sources. Please consult a licensed professional before attempting any techniques outlined in this Story.

By reading this document, the reader agrees that under no circumstances is the author responsible for any losses, direct or indirect, which are incurred as a result of the use of the information contained within this document, including, but not limited to, errors, omissions or inaccuracies.

This Story is a work of fiction. Any resemblance to actual person, living or dead, or actual events is entirely coincidental. Names, characters, businesses, organizations, places, events, and incidents are products of the author's imagination or are used fictitiously.

Table of Contents

Introduction

Thank you for choosing this guide.

If you have purchased this book, it is because you are looking for a simple clear and concise text that can train you carefully, using comprehensible language, and accompany you in the world of cryptocurrencies. Great, you are starting off on the right foot.

It is necessary to make a premise: investing is not a simple thing.

Before starting to put capital at stake, it is necessary to know very well the financial market, the trends, the forecasts provided by official sources and other materials of analysis. There are strong fluctuations in the world of financial markets and there always will be, no one can refrain from them, but on the other hand, it is also not as difficult as it seems. To be able to operate in the cryptocurrency market in fact, it is not necessary to have particular technical skills comparable to a Wall Street broker, but it is necessary to inform oneself and however to act with caution, to make weighted investments in relation to one's personal finances, especially in a digital currency market that is often subject to strong market fluctuations, sometimes bullish but sometimes very bearish.

To give you a sneak peek of the cryptocurrency market, let us take the queen of the market, namely Bitcoin (BTC), as a model and reference. Since its invention in 2009, this currency has undergone an amazing growth until 2017, when 1 bitcoin had reached the record amount of 20,000 US dollars. Over the next two years, the same coin had undergone a dizzying slump to reach a listing of around $8,000. As of today, early 2021, the coin has touched $50,000. Analysts speculate that the same coin could reach $100,000 by the end of 2021, but it is difficult to make concrete predictions.

Therefore, if you are not already an expert, in order to become a trader and an investor you must at least be extremely aware of what you are doing. It is fundamental to avoid diving into the void and gambling of any kind to avoid getting caught up in easy enthusiasms. It is fine to have funds and energy and to invest large sums of money in a very profitable market but being aware that it is still uncertain. Vice versa, to be taken by panic and fear if there is a bearish trend. The psychological and emotional factor has always played an important role on the markets, but we must be stronger, have the right approach and act as much as possible with knowledge and competence.

1. What Are Cryptocurrencies and How Do They Work?

Let us start by saying that cryptocurrencies are virtual currencies that allow for financial transactions thanks to complex cryptography that allows for the secure and anonymous generation, storage, and trading of a specific digital token.

Initially, cryptocurrencies were not born to be considered currencies, but they have become so over time.

Satoshi Nakamoto, the one who considers himself the inventor of Bitcoins, simply wanted to develop a peer-to-peer electronic cash system for sharing files.

Nakamoto, unlike all his predecessors, managed to prove that it was possible to have a cryptocurrency, without the need for a central authority.

In practice, thanks to the peer-to-peer system, when the transaction has taken place it will have to be confirmed by the miners. Only miners can confirm transactions. As long as a transaction is not confirmed, it can be forged. Instead, when it is confirmed, the transaction is no longer editable and enters the historical transactions, the so-called blockchain.

When a transaction has been confirmed by a miner, each node must add it to its database.

For this work, miners are rewarded with a cryptocurrency token. This method allows the system to operate securely and consistently over time.

A blockchain, for being clearer as possible, is a digital record of transactions. The name comes from its structure, in which individual records, called blocks, are linked together in single list, called a chain. Each transaction added to a blockchain is validated by multiple computers on the Internet.

2. How a Wallet Works?

It is quite simple. A Wallet / digital wallet creates and stores the private key (password) associated with a public key (address of the wallet / wallet).

Private keys are basically kept secret and never revealed as they allow you to spend money.

If the private key is lost, you can no longer access the wallet to make transactions or withdraw your coins.

This has been specified before, but I tend to want to voluntarily emphasize and reiterate fundamental concepts.

When we initiate a transaction with any cryptocurrency, all we do is subscribe ownership of the coins to the recipient's address (Public Key).

In a transaction, software creates a digital signature by processing the transaction using the private key. This makes it extremely secure as the only way to generate a valid signature for a specific transaction is to use the private key associated with it.

Each Wallet of any cryptocurrency is identified by a specific unique address (public key) consisting of 26 to 35 digits similar to an Iban.

The moment we request a payment, all we have to do is provide this address (public key) to the person who has to make the transaction on our account.

3. Seven Advantages and Three Disadvantages of Cryptocurrencies

7 Advantages of cryptocurrencies:

1) Since they are digital currencies and not "paper" money, they cannot be counterfeited.

2) The cost of transactions, if compared to that of physical and real coins, is much lower.

3) Since they are not subject to controls, every transaction and investment takes place in the complete protection of personal privacy.

4) Not being controlled by any central authority, the decentralized nature of the blockchain makes cryptocurrencies immune to the old ways of government control and interference.

5) Their number in circulation is limited, not infinite, therefore, their value is guaranteed.

6) Since it is a digital currency, you can send and receive money anywhere in the world, without worrying about limitations for traditional money transfer, such as borders or holidays.

7) Over time, more and more goods and services can be purchased all over the world using virtual currency, consolidating over time as an ordinary alternative payment method to the classic one.

3 Disadvantages of Cryptocurrencies:

1) The volatility of cryptocurrencies is a well-known and incontrovertible factor. These virtual currencies are subject to sudden rises or falls, from day to night. Therefore, the risk of losing a lot of money in the short term could be high if you adopt a highly speculative strategy in the short term.

2) To date, compared to traditional markets, there is still little information regarding the future of cryptocurrencies, and it

is still a rather nebulous world, so to speak. There is no single dictate regarding their development and consolidation plans. Every single digital currency is a story in itself and as a result, this scarcity of forecasting can create a strong and justified resistance from some investors to make transactions in this virtual market.

3) Despite the significant progress made to improve security, to date, hacker attacks remain frequent. If an investor does not take a whole series of precautions, he could easily be attacked and "robbed" of all his cryptocurrencies. For this reason, before being able to operate in the sector, it is necessary to raise your security level a lot.

4. The Step-by-Step Guide to Protect Your Cryptocurrencies from Hacker Attacks

If someone were to pull a bank robbery, your capital would still be safe as it is protected by the bank itself, right?

In turn, the financial institution has protected itself from any risks by taking out strict insurance policies.

The same thing happens if your credit card is cloned during a normal transaction. After having made a report to the competent authority, the bank will normally proceed to the regular refund of the amount unduly stolen.

But if I buy cryptocurrencies who protects me from hacker attacks?

The possibility that someone steals all your virtual currencies, unfortunately, is a very real and widespread hypothesis. Hacker attacks, as already anticipated, unfortunately remain very frequent.

This aspect is not much emphasized by bloggers or self-styled experts or completely glossed over by cryptocurrency buying portals, since they earn commissions on all transactions, because aspect could undermine the enthusiasm or hold back many investors.

However, one of the first and fundamental rules that one learns when becoming a trader or simple holder of digital currencies, is that it is we ourselves who must be the bank of our cryptocurrency. We are the ones who must protect our own treasure chest and personal treasure. It is crucial to never underestimate this aspect.

Step One

Make the password you use to access your computer complicated.

In fact, not just complicated, it needs to be extremely complicated, extremely difficult.

Forget about using the usual, simple, and trivial password you have been using for years for your personal emails or accounts linked to various platforms you are subscribed to. If you operate with the same email and for convenience you have stored it on the network, it will really be child's play for hackers to get into your computer. For them to steal capital from your virtual wallet will be like stealing candy from a baby or throwing a steak into a tank full of hungry sharks.

Use a new password, create one especially for the occasion and make sure you have never used it before. This password should be at least 20 characters long and consist of alternating letters, numbers, and special characters. Do not use sequences already used in other accounts or old emails or personal subscriptions. Eliminate birthdates, wedding anniversaries, names of children or pets, birthdays of relatives or friends, etc. nothing that can be traced back to your personal data and easily found through social networks or other sources.

This first trick will turn your password from weak to strong, making it overly complicated for outsiders to access your PC.

Remember, never forget, or underestimate this element. Not having an extremely difficult and strong password would be the same as not having a secure or locked door at home. A commonplace password, for example personal birth date plus dog's name, is equivalent to going to sleep or going out of the house leaving the door wide open.

Step Two

Install an anti-malware and start scanning consistently.

Anti-malware software provides protection against viruses and other types of malware, including Trojans, worms, and spyware. Basically, all you do is run a scan to detect programs that are malicious and eliminate "weeds from the field."

In particular, such programs (you can find many of them even free on the net), might detect a known malware, an unknown previous malware, or recent suspicious files that would be better not to download to your device.

Step Three

Adopt an encrypted e-mail and use it only for cryptocurrencies.

Another especially important step that should not be underestimated is to raise the security level of your email. This can happen thanks to an email called "encrypted", compared to a simple email.

This step is essential because, in order to access your profile or personal portfolio, regardless of the server you prefer, you will always be required to verify access and confirm your identity via email.

If someone could easily access your credentials, enter your computer device and access through your email on the portal where you usually buy, sell or exchange cryptocurrencies and to which your credit card and personal bank account are linked, the hacker in attack would only need a snap of his fingers to transfer all your virtual currencies.

Step Four

Set up a dual identity recognition method.

To access the portal that you have chosen and then the profile where you usually make transactions, make sure that the portal, in addition to sending you a confirmation email to your encrypted email, which you must confirm to have access, also sends a verification code to your smartphone, so that the portal is 100% sure that it is really you and that it is not a fake, who tries to illegally enter in your place in the profile.

In short, you need to make sure that you have the keys to your chest firmly in place.

Step Five

Buy a crypto wallet external to your portal.

A further strategy to shelter from external attacks of hackers and various scams, is to buy a crypto wallet (on average, a crypto wallet costs from 80 to 120 USD) where you can transfer all your cryptocurrencies as it is not recommended to leave them for a long time on the portal in your virtual wallet.

Hardware Wallets store a user's private keys on a hardware device like a USB pen drive. They can support multiple currencies. They are the most secure methods in the world, but they involve one big problem, if they break or you lose them, you will lose everything.

Step Six

Mark down with pen and paper on a personal planner, just in the most traditional of methods, all passwords and crypto wallet recovery codes.

As we have seen in the previous pages, to raise security it is essential to adopt passwords that are often complicated and difficult to keep in mind, nevertheless it applies to the various recovery codes of the crypto wallet.

Therefore, it is necessary to have a special diary (well, it would be much better to have two, where one serves as a backup of the first one) where you can jot down all the codes.

You should keep this diary like the famous briefcase that contains the nuclear codes and always travels with the President of the United States of America.

This is the most valuable advice I can give you.

It sounds like a joke, but in reality, it often happens to run into interviews with young neo multi-millionaire very proud to have bought Bitcoin in times when no one knew anything about it or believed in it, but who shows a very sad face because he can't find his crypto wallet or simply can't access it because he can't find his passwords anymore. It is not so difficult to suppose that he has absent-mindedly written them down who knows where, maybe on some piece of paper thrown away in the trash of the cafeteria underneath his house or stuck who knows where among other documents of 5 or 6 years, maybe in the storage of a rented apartment where he does not live anymore. Believe me, it is the pure truth. After all, many people started out almost as a joke or as a bet, underestimating the real scope of the investment. Recently an interview with an American guy with an estimated fortune of about 220 million USD (now quadrupled, given the current value of Bitcoins), who was unable to access his fortune, has been released in the press. This would be the drama, as well as the worst-case scenario, that could happen to an investor. Therefore, please always act like true professionals, protect yourself. File and handle everything with order, rigor, and precision.

Step Seven

Put your diaries and crypto wallet in a safe place.

Last but not the least step is to prevent someone from stealing your crypto wallet or your password diary. Therefore, keep them in a safe place, where only you or extremely trusted people (usually no more than one or two people, never enlarge the circle) can access them.

In essence, using a further metaphor, imagine you are in ancient Egypt and you must use all the tricks, (secret tunnels, deceptive writing, walled rooms, and passages that lead off course) so that no thief inside the Pyramid can access the tomb of Pharaoh and loot all the gold. Think for example of the incredibly famous tomb of Pharaoh Tutankhamun. Only the sarcophagus containing the mummy, made of solid gold, given the value of the same to the ounce, in correspondence of its weight is worth about 40 million U.S. dollars. Now this priceless treasure is in the Cairo museum along with the funeral mask of the deceased young ruler, priceless artifacts that were found along with other precious objects and furnishings. If this unique patrimony in the world, not only for its economic value but also for its historical value, had not been found in 1922 by the English archaeologist Howard Carter but by one of the many grave robbers, it would have been lost and would not be admired by the whole of humanity.

Summary of How to Protect Your Cryptocurrencies from Hacker Attacks

- 1 Make the password you use to access your computer complicated.
- 2 Install an anti-malware and start scanning consistently.
- 3 Adopt an encrypted e-mail and use it only for cryptocurrencies.

- 4 Set up a dual identity recognition method.
- 5 Buy a crypto wallet external to your portal.
- 6 Mark down with pen and paper on a personal planner, just in the most traditional of methods, all passwords and crypto wallet recovery codes.
- 7 Put your diaries and crypto wallet in a safe place.

5. Where to Start Buying Cryptocurrencies to Create Your Own Asset

In case the person who is reading the content of this book is already an expert, this paragraph for might be superfluous or merely informative. If, on the other hand, you know nothing about cryptocurrencies, have never traded, are new to the industry and want to start operating in this new field, first, you need to look for a marketplace that is serious and reliable where you can start buying cryptocurrencies.

The marketplace is a place where you can usually have a prior view of the prices, have a view of the charts where you can freely and easily monitor the trend of the last hour, the last 24 hours, the last week, the last month or even the last year.

Analyzing the trend several times a day and at different times, can definitely be a good habit to follow, taking into account that the cryptocurrency market is global, given that there are time zones, and you cannot physically monitor the currency 24 hours a day.

The most important exchange marketplaces are Coinbase, Kraken, Bittrex, Cryptopia, Binance or Coinmama.

What can differentiate one marketplace from another, in essence, are the commissions that the platform might use when you make transactions.

Personally, for beginners, I recommend using Coinbase because it is the simplest, most intuitive and clear. Once you become an expert or have a solid confidence, then you can, if you want, move to other exchanges more "sophisticated" and less intuitive.

First you will need to register. In this regard, before starting the registration process and performing various operations, I recommend that you follow the instructions in the previous chapter "**4. The Step-by-Step Guide to Protect Your Cryptocurrencies from Hacker Attacks**".

Coinbase will ask you to fill out all the fields with your personal references, tax data, as well as any ordinary registration you are used to doing.

After creating your profile, you will then need to tie in your credit card or rechargeable card in to be able to buy cryptocurrency.

You will also need to add your bank account details, should you decide to transfer your money from your Coinbase wallet to your personal bank account.

When you have set up your entire profile, all that is left to do is to give you an overview of virtual coins, with their constantly updated market price.

I strongly recommend that you **never save your password**, even if your browser recommends it (so that your password does not remain fixed on the web and can be captured by some hacker using malware) and always make sure you have done **Exit / Logout** from your profile once you have finished operating on the portal.

These are simple tips, but believe me, extremely crucial for your personal and financial security.

Each cryptocurrency will have a dedicated line among the various of the list, inside, you will find all the data and the most relevant information.

If the currency is growing, in correspondence of the price of the same you will find a percentage of green color (for example +0.45%) if the price is rising, or a percentage of red color (for example -0.45%) if the price is falling.

Also, on the main screen you will be shown, by averaging, if in general the cryptocurrency market is up or down, and it will indicate you the relative percentage.

This overview can give you a generic and non-specific indicator on what the market trend is.

On Coinbase you will find the list of a lot of virtual coins, but beware, not on all of them you will be able to perform operations (mainly on all the most relevant ones, that is). The exchange portal reserves the right to operate only on some that it considers important, or it may reserve, for security, instability, or other reasons not to deal with them.

If the portal allows you to deal with a coin, then you will find a blue button in its corresponding row with the words "make transactions". At that point, you can buy the currency by entering the amount in dollars or euros you wish to invest.

Once you enter the amount of 20, 30, 100 USD, you will be shown the indicated cryptocurrency amount. For example, if the coin has a value of 1 USD and you invest 100 USD you will have and find in your personal portfolio, inside the exchange 100 cryptocurrencies of that coin.

If instead you decide to invest 100 USD in a cryptocurrency that is worth 40,000, as in the case of Bitcoin, you will have on your personal profile a percentage of Bitcoin corresponding to 100 USD. In this case, therefore, you will have 0.0025 Bitcoin on deposit.

Once you have built your portfolio of cryptocurrencies you can decide to sell them or alternatively exchange them with other cryptocurrencies, if you realize that there are some coins that perform better than others, or if you notice any positive or negative trends.

Exchanges usually between virtual coins are not subject to commissions, while if you buy or sell, usually the marketplace takes a percentage (which is the main source of income of the said platform, it is obvious). Once converted, you will find on your personal wallet the new dollar or euro amount updated at the cryptocurrency's conversion rate.

All you have to do is type in the "transfer" option; again, you can decide whether to transfer the entire amount in dollars, euros, or just a part of the sum. At this point you will just have to indicate among the options your bank account or your credit card, after that, your transfer will be immediate. If you decide to leave a part of the capital in dollars or euros on the platform, you can use them later to buy directly from your Coinbase wallet other cryptocurrencies, without having to buy or withdraw money from your credit card.

I always recommend, to never leave high amounts of either cryptocurrencies or dollars or euros on your personal wallet on your exchange, because beyond all the precautions you could take, you are never completely safe from hacker attacks. Therefore, I always recommend transferring large amounts to a crypto or hard wallet for further protection.

6. Five Cryptocurrency Parameters to Analyze Before Investing in Cryptocurrencies

1. Charts, Supports and Resistances.

Exceptionally useful in understanding the future of a cryptocurrency especially in the short term are the so-called supports and resistances. These are chart-type trading indicators that can be used by simply plotting them on the chart.

- A **support** represents a market share that the price fails to overcome on the downside, causing bullish rebounds.

- A **resistance** is a market share which the price fails to overcome on the upside, causing bearish rebounds.

In practice, supports and resistances in trading are areas of the chart that the price struggles to overcome. These are technical concepts that are a bit difficult to understand, especially for beginners, but through a visual analysis of the charts these parameters are easier to understand in practice than in theory. Summarizing and resuming the above concepts, a support is the area of the chart where the price, in the past, has not been able to overcome downwards. A resistance instead is the area of the chart where the price, in the past, was not able to go upwards. In essence, they are indicators to understand the minimum and maximum price of a currency and serve to understand the bullish or bearish trend of the cryptocurrency.

Analyzing the charts of virtual currencies, as for the trading market, is an important and fundamental factor to analyze the trend of a virtual currency. Making an analysis also through the relative trend of the last hour, the last day, the last week, the last month and finally the whole year can make understand what the market trend regarding the cryptocurrency is.

A detailed analysis, compared to a random investment with no logic, is highly recommended, even if it is always a market subject to strong fluctuations and totally unpredictable.

2. Technological Changes.

Another strategic aspect to keep in mind and that could lead over time to a fluctuation of the virtual currency and its eventual increase in value are certainly the technological development processes and innovations that the currency itself intends to adopt. One example was the transition from Ethereum to Ethereum 2.0. expected from 2020, or the integration of the Ripple cryptocurrency into Amazon's payment system.

3. Commercial Acceptance.

The more commercial a currency becomes, the more trust in it grows. The fact that a cryptocurrency becomes in the mind of the community of common use, increases the reliability and trust in the same exponentially (it is a law as old as the world and applicable to many fields). For example, the fact that Elon Musk has publicly declared that Tesla's electric cars can be paid for in the short term with Bitcoins only strengthens the position of this virtual currency, with an increase in value given to a consequent mass market interest.

4 Law of The Market.

The market price is given by supply and demand. When it is born, a virtual currency has a great availability, but perhaps a low desirability on the market. This oscillation between supply and demand means that the market price is exceptionally low. As the availability is scarce, since virtual currencies are issued in limited numbers, and there is a lot of interest in a particular currency, the logical consequence will be a real surge in value, because there will be a real chase after gold to get the largest number of cryptocurrencies.

5 Media and World News.

Events or news in the public domain can influence the market trend and by no small amount. All the excitement related to cryptocurrencies at the beginning of 2021 is linked to the fact that many institutional players and numerous billionaires have begun to invest heavily in this market. Obviously, this causes a ripple effect or emulation effect (i.e to be clear, the average saver tries to move by following those figures they consider authoritative. Translated, the logical thought is: "if they invest, who know and are competent, surely it is a good deal"). Vice versa, a negative news, such as a decision like the one of the SEC to sue Ripple can generate a negative effect and a total escape on other cryptocurrencies, fearing a real collapse of the same. As was the case with the 1929 crisis and as British economist John Maynard Keynes, one of the most influential economists of the 20th century and father macroeconomics explained that one of the main causes of the great Wall Street crisis was largely due to "Negative Expectations". The confidence of entrepreneurs in the economic recovery in 1929 was minimal, negative expectations pushed entrepreneurs to postpone to the future their productive investments (animal spirits), further distancing the conditions to get out of the economic depression.

Summary:

1. Charts, Supports and Resistances.

2. Technological Changes.

3. Commercial Acceptance.

4 Law of The Market.

5 Media and World News.

7. How to choose the Best Cryptocurrencies to Bet on in the Short and Long Term?

As of June 2020, there are an estimated 2,677 types of cryptocurrencies.

They pop up like mushrooms in the fall, don't they?

The question you may be asking yourself is: which cryptocurrency is worth investing in? And: which cryptocurrency will have a higher return?

Well, to answer these questions with absolute certainty you would need to possess a powerful magic orb or any prophecy. I remind you that, as anticipated in the previous chapters, the cryptocurrency market is characterized by strong fluctuations. Strong volatility sometimes corresponds in sudden peaks of gains but also in dizzying collapses, most often subject to unpredictability or mere speculative actions of large brokers who move huge amounts of cryptocurrency. High volatility often translates into high risk, especially if you are not a professional player or at least people who are informed and have some experience in the financial sector.

I would like to underline once again the importance of investing an amount of money commensurate with your financial capabilities. This approach is valid not only in the beginning, but also for the future. It is usually advisable to invest an amount not exceeding 10% of your capital. This is a sum that, if it were to fall short suddenly, would not put you and your personal finances in trouble.

As far as the type of investor is concerned, it is undeniable that there are and always will be those who are more unscrupulous, those who are thriftier and those who seek to make the maximum profit in the short term. Some people like to earn through immediate and continuous speculation, while others prefer to think and dress in cryptocurrencies in the long run, believing deeply in the project and the work that the creators of the virtual currency are doing. There is no single way of being or investing, and none of these can actually be called the most correct. The last type of investor mentioned, however, is the one related to those who are used to buy virtual currencies and then set them aside, almost forgetting them for years, without being influenced positively or negatively by the fluctuations of quotations, and maybe finding themselves with excellent results after a decade.

Having said that, if on the one hand it is not predictable to know the future trend of a virtual currency, on the other hand, information, market movements of the main players, information sites, forecasts of people working in the sector (even if often they are not totally impartial, for this reason it is always better to get information and make comparisons on an increasing number of sources), graphs and experience can help to understand or at least hypothesize if a cryptocurrency can have a bullish or bearish push or can have growth prospects in the future or if the project is not yet ready to take off or will never take off.

Usually, cryptocurrency investors, before betting or not on a virtual currency, try to understand the path that the founders of the currency want to take and what their concrete project is.

Often the mission of the cryptocurrency emerges directly from the "**White Paper**", a term often used and inflated in this market sector. White Papers are technical documents, publications where reflections, opinions or orientations are indicated.

Brief historical note: where does the term "White" come from?

The term was coined in Britain in the 1950s, when the British government wanted to distinguish shorter, more concise research with a white cover from more detailed research that had a blue cover instead.

Crypto investors often use the **POPER** method, which is an acronym where **P** stands for "**Problem**", O stands for "**Opportunity**", **P** stands for "**Plan**", **E** stands for "**Experience**", **R** stands for "**Results**".

The Poper method seeks to analyze a project by answering critical questions: What **problem** will the company solve? Is the **opportunity** big enough? Is the **plan** to solve the problem good enough? Does the team have the **experience** to carry out the plan? What will the **results** look like?

Personally, I think everyone can unearth some remarkably interesting coins, which in my humble opinion should be viewed or analyzed more carefully than others.

In addition to the queen of cryptocurrencies, **Bitcoin**, to the consolidation of **Etherum** which performed a +700% or so in 2020, effectively becoming Bitcoin's main antagonist, I find it interesting to analyze coins such as: **Chainlink**, **Yearn**, **Finance** and **Litcoin**. I would definitely keep an eye on **Monero** as well, and in the long run-on **BNB** and **Enjin**.

I repeat and emphasize that this is only a recommendation based on data analyzed in a limited time segment and by me individually, so everything cannot be evaluated objectively, but subjectively, as the market is unpredictable. Everyone must and is free to make their own evaluations regarding the best form of investment of their capital in relation to the own budget and the historical period, as well as financial, that one is facing.

We will analyze in detail the single Cryptocurrencies in the next chapter.

8. Bitcoin, What Maximum Amount Will It Reach?

Although everyone knows this currency, as if it were the Picasso in the art world, that is, a name known even to the non-expert, it is right and proper to make a minimum of premise.

Bitcoin (abbreviated as BTC) is the first open-source and peer-to-peer digital cryptocurrency, released in 2008 by a programmer, or group of programmers (the matter is deliberately kept secret and ambiguous) independent known as Satoshi Nakamoto. The digital currency does not use any centralized server for issuing, transaction processing and storage; instead, it makes use of a new technology, a public distributed database called Blockchain. The network makes use of electronic signatures and is supported by a Proof-of-Work protocol, which guarantees the security and legitimacy of monetary transactions. The issuance of Bitcoin is done by the users themselves through a process called mining, and the maximum monetary supply is limited to 21 million units.

In 2021, this cryptocurrency touched the 50,000 USD threshold and everyone is wondering where it will go in the short term and especially in the medium to long term.

Will BTC reach stellar figures or is it a real speculative bubble?

Elon Musk, a successful South African entrepreneur with Canadian citizenship naturalized U.S. Founder, CEO and CTO of Space Exploration Technologies Corporation, co-founder, CEO and product architect of Tesla, and co-founder and CEO of Neuralink, he led the way with his $1.5 billion investment in Bitcoin. Many seem interested in following in the Tesla founder's footsteps, including Bank of New York Mellon, Mastercard, Morgan Stanley and Deutsche Bank. With the end of 2020 and the beginning of the year 2021, the excitement is skyrocketing and and according to some analysts, the price of the currency could go much higher still.

Among the first analysts to set Bitcoin's next target at 70 thousand USD was Simon Peters, cryptocurrency expert from the **eToro Platform**. According to the expert, the fact that an increasing number of multinationals are attracted to Bitcoin, could turn 70 thousand USD quota into the new normal of the said cryptocurrency.

According to Peters, Bitcoin is driving an upheaval in the status quo by "capitalizing on the waning power of the dollar." While the Greenback is showing continued signs of fatigue, the value of Bitcoin is growing.

In this context, the eToro analyst concluded, there is no reason "why the 70,000 USD cannot soon become the new normality." Indeed, always according to the expert, 70 thousand level is not to be intended as a new target because nothing excludes that there may be rises even above this level.

Many analysts believe that investing in cryptocurrencies and in particular BTCs would be a viable alternative to hedge against inflation.

According to Anthony Pompliano, co-founder of Morgan Creek Digital Assets, bitcoin could touch 500,000 USD and then double in the long run.

Honestly, I do not know if this prediction can be considered realistic or a bit too optimistic and pumped up.

Certainly, the high volatility of the price of the asset could, as on a real roller coaster, undergo significant ups and downs, given a still too high share of retail investors.

All that remains is to carefully examine the charts and monitor the trend of the queen of cryptocurrencies.

9. Will Ethereum, With Version 2.0, Become Like Bitcoins?

Ethereum 2.0: What it is and How it Works.

Just like Bitcoin, Ethereum uses proof of work as a consensus mechanism to ensure maximum decentralization.

The main limitations arising from this use are: latency (the time interval between the sending of a transaction and its registration on the Blockchain), throughput (the amount of transactions per unit of time) and high energy consumption.Much of the research activity in the field of permissionless platforms, is directed to find solutions to ensure the scalability of these networks without compromising security and decentralization.

But unlike other blockchains, the Ethereum cryptocurrency can do so much more. It is programmable, so developers can use it to create new types of applications.

These decentralized applications (called "dapps") take advantage of the benefits of cryptocurrencies and blockchain technology. They are trusted because, once they are "uploaded" to Ethereum, they always run according to how they were programmed. They can control digital assets to create new types of financial applications. They can be decentralized, meaning no individual or legal entity controls them.

Even at this very moment, thousands of developers around the world are certainly creating Ethereum-based applications and inventing new types, many of which are already usable. For example:

- Cryptocurrency wallets that allow you to make instant, inexpensive payments with ETH or other assets.

- Financial applications that allow you to borrow, lend or invest digital assets.

- Decentralized markets that allow you to trade digital assets, or even make "predictions" about events in the real world.

- Games where the player owns the objects in the game and can even earn money.

Now, thanks to this upgrade, the consensus protocol will pass from proof of work to proof of stake, a mechanism in which the block validator is not chosen with probability proportional to the computational work performed but based on a combination of the amount of value possessed, the time for which it has been maintained and the willingness of the validators to put it in "play" (at stake). The proof of stake would have the great advantage of allowing a considerable increase in performance, together with an infinitely higher energy efficiency.

Phase 0 focuses on the activation of Ethereum's new Proof of Stake system, Casper. Validators in Phase 0 will work to protect the backbone of the Ethereum 2.0 system known as the "beacon chain," and that is the "central blockchain" that will create a registry of all Ethereum 2.0 validators, their stake, and assign their roles. At this stage, all existing users and dapps will continue to send their transactions on the Ethereum PoW blockchain as normal.

Phase 0 of Ethereum 2.0

The creation of the beacon chain will represent the initial phase (for this reason called Phase 0) towards the implementation of sharding, that is the fragmentation of the main chain into sub-chains (the shards), in which it is possible to perform internal validations, with the consequent advantage of parallelizing the creation of blocks and therefore increasing the total throughput of the network. At the same time, the size of the state that the validator nodes must maintain in memory decreases, and therefore the number of devices able to take part in the verification and validation process increases.

10. Can Litecoin Be the Alternative to Ethereum?

Litecoin (abbreviated LTC) was born in 2011 thanks to the idea of a former Googler and MIT graduate, Charlie Lee.

Despite its innovative potential, Litecoin has lost ample ground to the Ethereum boom but still continues to boast a certain prestige in the cryptocurrency market.

The incentive for miners is 50 Litecoin per successfully verified block. Every 2.5 minutes the network generates a so-called block that is added to the others and with them goes to make up the blockchain, the public register of all transactions in Litecoin.

The number of Litecoin in circulation has already been established at the time of its creation: the limit is 84 million.

What makes Litecoin better than Bitcoin, according to its creator, are the possibilities of being able to reach a greater number of virtual wallets and the higher limit (84 million against Bitcoin's 21 million).

Another distinctive element are the mining times of Litecoin: four times less than those for Bitcoin. Litecoin takes 2.5

minutes to generate a block, while Bitcoin takes at least 10 minutes.

A third Bitcoin-Litecoin difference can also be traced in the algorithm used by cryptocurrencies. Litecoin uses Scrypt which, being a sequential memory-hard function requires more memory.

Surely, this virtual currency has also made a significant leap forward in 2020 and 2021. Making growth predictions is always risky, but it is certainly to be considered an established cryptocurrency with a good project behind it.

11. Why Monero Is NOT Trusted by Some Exchange Platforms?

Monero (XMR) is for all intents and purposes one of the most popular cryptocurrencies, yet it does not enjoy great trust from some marketplaces, so much so that they have decided not to list it. Why this choice?

Let us go into the merits of the story.

A brief historical intro is necessary. Monero was born in April 2014. Initially, it was called BitMonero, and then it became simply Monero over time.

Unlike many other cryptocurrencies that are derived from Bitcoin, Monero is based on the CryptoNight protocol, a derivative of the CryptoNote algorithm and has significant algorithmic differences on Blockchain obfuscation.

This specific virtual currency uses cryptographic and technical gimmicks that it makes use of to hide sensitive details (amount, identity, and address of users), resulting in making it an untraceable cryptocurrency.

Known as the cryptocurrency characterized by the highest level of anonymity, it is called by industry experts as "privacy coin".

This rigidity regarding privacy has made this type of virtual currency among the most used to carry out criminal activities in the dark web, but also to carry out illicit activities to the detriment of other cryptocurrency users.

How do cryptocurrency scams work? It is necessary, again, to briefly introduce, trying to simplify and make it as understandable as possible, the concept of "double spending".

It takes time to update the Blockchain nodes and in that time frame, albeit minimal, the same cryptocurrency is spent on more than one transaction.

The most common way to make a "double spending" is to send in the Blockchain two transactions in rapid succession (so-called "race attack").

Another method of "double spending" is the Finney one in which the miner, while waiting for the pre-mining, spends the same coins before releasing the "block" in the Blockchain, and then invalidate that transaction.

Beyond money laundering, Monero also lends itself to direct attacks: in July 2020, a *ransomware* encrypted all the corporate files of an Argentine telephone company, and then demanded as much as 218 thousand XMR, an amount equal to about 15 million USD. Recall that without an encryption key, it is almost impossible to recover this data and the only way to decrypt the files is to pay the ransom.

Given the lack of transparency related to XMR, Brain Armstrong, another "Rockstar" in the crypto world, as well as founder of Coinbase, which we mentioned earlier among the main exchange platforms dedicated to cryptocurrencies, has declared, and decided not to list Monero on his platform due to " a problem with regulators".

Other cryptocurrency exchanges such as South Korean Bithumb and Singaporean exchange HUOBI have also decided to remove Monero from their platforms.

12. Yearn.Finance (YFI) Beta Project or Solid Reality?

How can you not talk about Yearn.Finance (abbreviated YFI), given that just two months after its launch in February 2020, on a project by Andre Cronje, it went from 0 to 38,000 USD?

How can we not talk about a platform that has performed in the last year + 3,759.09 %?

The answer is amazingly simple, it is inevitable to talk about it and make so much analysis on it.

Let us consider that, just to give a term of comparison, on average, leaving our money on the current account, when we are lucky, they indicate in clear letters, as if it were the deal of the century, makes us an interest of 2% per year. Obviously, it must be considered gross, given the various management costs that current accounts have. But surely if you are reading this book a certain way of investing, traditional strategies to be clear, is not what you are looking for.

Here is a better understanding of how this works. I will try to simplify as much as possible, to make the concept usable even if exhaustive for those who are not experts or already have experience in the field.

Yearn.finance is a decentralized finance platform that performs several functions such as leveraged trading, aggregated liquidity, and automated market maker.

yEarn Finance (YFI) is a DeFi (decentralized finance) yield aggregator on Ethereum. The platform offers cryptocurrency holders the ability to take part in "yield farming" or, literally translated, "agricultural production" (i.e., creating tokens).

In essence, the yearn.finance platform offers the opportunity for cryptocurrency holders to participate in yield farming by interacting with DeFi protocols. The farming process resembles the usual planting of seeds in the ground to multiply them.To harvest DeFi from the yearn.finance platform, you must block (place a bet) in cryptocurrency. YFI virtual tokens are distributed among platform members as a reward.

The Yearn Finance (YFI) platform is a kind of yield aggregator - via the iEarn "Y" pool (yPool). The protocol automatically invests funds escrowed by users in various DeFi projects, choosing those with the highest yield and ROI.

These funds are then transferred to the various protocols that offer the best rates of return, including Compound, Aave, and dYdX.

How does the undermining occur on YFI? The Yearn Finance (YFI) token is not created through traditional mining on ASICs or video cards but can be acquired by investing in the project. So, specifically, first you must buy one of the cryptocurrencies that supports the Yearn Finance protocol, send the purchased tokens towards one of the pools, and then get the reward in YFI.

The YFI cryptocurrency is a token of the ERC-20 (Ethereum) standard and is supported by MEW, Metamask, and other apps that allow the deposit of Ethereum (ERC-20) tokens.

YFI Long-Term Price Forecast

No one can predict the future of any cryptocurrency.

However, we can show you the possible prediction for YFI token.

Year	Wallet Investor	Digital Currency Price
2021	$ 309.300	$ 58.800
2022	$ 323.000	$ 81.500
2023	$ 570.000	$ 86.300
2024	$ 740.000	$ 115.000
2025	$ 960.000	$ 131.000

As can be seen from the chart, the forecast is bullish. I would not be so sure. I will reiterate once again that the cryptocurrency market is highly unpredictable. Therefore, it is crucial to conduct thorough research before investing in any cryptocurrency.

13. Why Buy Binance Coin?

The Binance Coin (BNB) is the cryptocurrency on the Binance exchange platform. Recently, this coin has attracted wide interest as it is the cryptocurrency on the world's largest cryptocurrency exchange by number of daily transactions.

Binance is derived from two words "Binary" and "Finance". This virtual currency was born in 2017 by ChangPeng Zhao, who founded a company called Beijie Technology, which is currently based in Hong Kong, and is the holding company that manages Binance.

Instead of creating an entirely new project, Binance chose to back its new project on the Ethereum blockchain. As we have analyzed in previous chapters, the Ethereum network was created specifically to be able to launch other decentralized tokens, apps, sites, and services.

Purchasing BNB can be done directly on the Binance exchange or on other marketplaces like eToro.

In two years, BNB (Binance Coin) has managed to accumulate an impressive market capitalization and enter the top 10 cryptocurrencies measured by that metric.

Binance Coin's primary functions are 3:

1) Acts as a cryptocurrency for investments.

2) It reduces fees on the Binance platform.

3) It is used to pay for assets on sites that accept Binance Coin.

To understand the real value of Binance Coin we shall quickly trace its growth:

- BNB started with a listing of USD 0.1 at launch.

- By the end of the year it had already reached USD 2 which became USD 20 in January 2018.

- In 2018 there was a drop to USD 10, but by then it had attracted many new investors and the value started to grow again and then dropped again at the end of the year touching USD 4.

- In 2019 the value of Binance Coin reached USD 39 and its market capitalization exceeded USD 5 Billion.

- 2020 was a continuous growth despite the retracement due to the coronavirus pandemic that did not spare even this cryptocurrency.

In the first months of 2021, its value is around USD 185. Definitely a good result.

I think this virtual currency is interesting and deserves to be monitored and followed carefully.

14. Chainlink: How Much Can Google's Choice Affect This Coin?

Chainlink is blockchain that aims to make processes more secure and efficient in industry, finance and contracting.

The latest news about Chainlink is that Google has also chosen to adopt its technology for Google Cloud applications. If the web giant has moved towards this crypto, surely the thing can only be extremely interested.

Around Chainlink revolves the LINK token, whose value has been growing for several years.

Chainlink is a cryptocurrency that aims to incentivize a global network of computers to provide reliable real-time data to Smart Contracts loaded on blockchain.

The Chainlink project was launched in June 2017 by SmartContract, a for-profit company based in the Cayman Islands. The founders of the company are Steve Ellis and Sergey Nazarov.

Properly, Chainlink is a decentralized network of nodes that provides data and information from off-blockchain sources to smart contracts on the blockchain. The process is done through a network of oracles, i.e., checking and validating nodes.

Chainlink is a decentralized network that receives, processes, and delivers data to contracts on the blockchain. Smart contracts are pre-made agreements (rules) that are automatically executed if and only if certain conditions are met.

Chainlink nodes, are called oracle or middleware. They act as intermediaries, in the middle between off-chain data and smart contracts and have the task of translating information coming from the outside into the language of contracts on the blockchain and vice versa.

What value can Chainlink achieve?

This is the most difficult answer to give as you would have to have a crystal ball or the machine from "Back to The Future" and be Michael J. Fox!

According to experts, LINK could touch a value above USD 45 by the 2021-22 biennium. According to Coinpedia, for example, Chainlink's value will see an exponential development by the end of 2025, which could be around USD 150 per token.

But these are just predictions. I always recommend not to make too reckless investments, as the market is always subject to high volatility.

15. Dogecoin: The Coin of The Funny Dog Born as a Joke.

Dogecoin is a cryptocurrency whose logo refers graphically to an Internet meme representing a dog breed Shiba Inu, in other words, like that dog in the famous Hollywood movie starring Richard Gere, named "Hachi: A Dog's Tale", which became famous because it is based on a true story of the Japanese dog named Hachikō (Hachi which in Japanese means eight, and the protagonist is called so because of a wooden tag worn around his neck in which is represented the number 8 in Japanese characters).

Gere plays the Japanese character of Hidesaburō Ueno, and the special relationship with his dog.

For those who have never seen it, it is definitely a film to see, very emotional. I will stop here so as not to make any kind of spoilers and to refocus on the cryptocurrency with the dog logo.

Born as a joke on December 8 in 2013, it quickly develops a community and in January 2014 reaches a market capitalization of USD 60 million. In June 2017, it has already reached a capitalization of USD 340 million and in January 2018 it reaches over USD 1 billion.

The cryptocurrency Dodgecoin, at the beginning of 2021, exponentially multiplied in value in the cryptocurrency market, causing a boom in interest in the topic. One of the platforms that allows you to buy dogecoin, is Kraken.

Dogecoin today boasts a prestigious position in the panorama of cryptocurrencies, with very considerable numbers both in terms of capitalization and in the number of exchanges: it is a peer-to-peer cryptocurrency, that is founded on a network in which each person connected acts as both client and server, and is based on Blockchain, a widespread data structure which is considered a kind of digital ledger.

It can be said without a doubt that Dogecoin has been able to turn out to be a very good marketing stunt, especially at the time of its foundation, when Jackson Palmer's cryptocurrency made people smile both for its logo and for its name.

The gimmick of enhancing the Doge dog turned out to be more than apt, then, but in addition to this it must be recognized that Dogecoin has engaged in effective marketing activities even after starting up.

Dogecoin marketing has often been related to philanthropy, and it can be said without any hesitation that the community of this cryptocurrency really has a great sensitivity towards the most deserving causes.

There are 4 main fundraising campaigns implemented by the Dogecoin community, some of which are very admirable on a humanitarian level, others equally laudable, but also more suggestive.

Here, specifically, are the 4 fundraising campaigns:

- 2014 Winter Olympics.

- Doge4Water.

- NASCAR.

- Doge4Family House.

The first funded the Jamaican bobsled team to take them to the Olympics, the second to build a water reservoir on the Tana River in Kenya, the third to support Nascar driver Josh Wise while the fourth is an effort to increase funding for the Family House association in California. The goal is to reach 1,500,000 Dogecoins that will be donated directly to Family House once the achievement is made.

Regarding this virtual currency, through numerous industry articles, news has spread that one person, or one legal entity, owns about 28% of all the new cryptocurrency in circulation, a share worth about USD 2.1 billion at current prices. Therefore, given the canine nature attached to this cryptocurrency, there has been joking talk of a real and proper top dog.

Dogecoin rose in popularity after well-known business and pop culture icons, including Tesla CEO Elon Musk, rapper Soulja Boy and "Malcolm in the Middle" star Frankie Muniz, also began promoting it online.

What is the connection between Game Stop and the cryptocurrency Dogecoin?

Well, it happened that on Reddit, an online platform for social news, entertainment, and forum container, where registered users can publish content in the form of textual posts or hyperlinks, an initiative was born to save Game Stop, a U.S. video games company that was going through a difficult period and was in danger of closing.

Within a few days, a forum brings together millions of people, the goal is to gather as many people as possible ready to invest in Game Stop shares, aimed precisely at saving the company. The result is incredible: almost six million people invest in masse from there to the following days, leading to an increase in the value of the shares, which from about USD 4 in 2020 shoots up to USD 500.

This happens on Thursday, January 28, 2021 and sends the entire investment sector into turmoil: the boom in prices makes "redditors" (as defined by the users of the Reddit forum that started it all) earn huge amounts of money and, as a result, a chain effect is generated that has seen the value of other stocks increase (such as BlackBerry and AMC), until it overwhelms Dogecoin, cryptocurrency whose existence dates back to some time ago but that today has returned to the fore.

In essence, we have witnessed a real fight between "David" and "Goliath", where individual users have decided, joining forces, to challenge the financial market, going against the odds, creating a bullish wave, and creating not a little confusion and noise on the traditional market. Many small gamers, many nostalgic lovers of the Game Stop chain, a familiar place, have become active with a sort of virtual crowdfunding to save the stores. You can really say that sometimes "union is strength!".

The price of Dogecoin rose by more than 900% in early 2021 to 5 cents apiece, so its shares went from a value of USD 0.007 (EUR 0.005 cents) to EUR 5.3 cents. This makes the market worth about USD 6.9 billion and puts the share of its largest owner at about USD 2.1 billion. Like bitcoin, dogecoin is created by a process known as mining: people solve complex mathematical puzzles using computers to unlock new coins.

What is the future of Dogecoin?

Can it be considered a virtual currency to bet on?

Elon Musk, CEO of SpaceX and Tesla has posted several tweets criticizing so-called micro-communities that hoard large stocks of nascent cryptocurrencies, effectively preventing their organic growth. Among them is Dogecoin which, according to Musk, can become truly mainstream, with a bit of a push to get started. A push that Musk himself will give it.

In unsuspected times, Musk himself said that Dogecoin could become the "people's cryptocurrency", the official currency on Mars: "If the main holders of Dogecoin sell most of their coins, it will get my full support. Too much focus is the only real problem," he wrote on Twitter.

The criticalities related to this cryptocurrency have been highlighted by its founder, the already mentioned Jackson Palmer.

Palmer affirms, in fact, that for this cryptocurrency born for fun, but then turned out to be a great success, there are no innovations of a technical nature, so it will not be easy for Dogecoin to keep up with the competition.

The picture that Palmer seems to outline is that of a cryptocurrency that could become obsolete and that, for this reason, could see its use collapse until it exits the market completely.

Many insiders do not believe much in this virtual currency. Personally, I do not have much confidence in this currency, but we are watching and monitoring what the future holds for us.

16. Why Ripple Keeps Not Exploding?

It is a very curious fact, in my opinion, despite the high euphoria related to the world of cryptocurrencies, that one of the historical currencies like Ripple (XRP) continues not to explode, as it happened to all the others.

Just do a brief historical introduction and presentation to better frame this virtual currency: Ripple, also known by the name of its currency XRP, was born in 2013, founded by Chris Larsen and Jed McCaleb and based on a protocol created by OpenCoin. At the basis of its birth, the desire of the founders to eliminate some disadvantages in the use of Bitcoin; needless to say, since Ripple is a cryptocurrency, there is no physical currency, but its value is based on monetary relationships that are exchanged only online.

Ripple's exchange protocol is managed by the company itself and is called Ripple Transaction Protocol, with which it is possible to exchange the XRP cryptocurrency in an easier way and with practically zero commissions. The database on which transactions are carried out through an algorithm called Ripple Consensus is called Ripple Consensus Ledger (RLC). The latter is able to offer immutability of transactions and was created in such a way to facilitate transactions across the network.

XRP is considered an atypical cryptocurrency. This is because Ripple is partly a bank-related system, which distances it from the classic concept of "virtual currency".

However, although Ripple is frowned upon by cryptocurrency purists, such a situation brings several advantages, such as a more stable market value, a feature that facilitates the adoption of XRPs at different levels, starting with banks and ending with other types of banking institutions.

In other words, unlike classic cryptocurrencies such as Bitcoin or Ethereum, Ripple has a form of centralization, or rather management by a central body. So, it is not a completely free project.

The Ripple project is an extremely ambitious idea. The creators of the platform aim to change the banking system as we know it. Ripple in fact proposes itself as an alternative to the SWIFT system.

SWIFT is nothing more than a banking intermediary that does not hold accounts or payments, but only acts as an intermediary. Ripple's goal, as opposed to SWIFT, is to offer much cheaper and faster money transfers than ever before.

So, we strongly wonder, why has Ripple suffered significant declines and why is it still not exploding?

Behind this coin's lack of growth, there appears to be a technical reason or cause. Even in the cryptocurrency sector, not everything comes about by chance, but even savers can be influenced by positive or negative market news and related trends.

Faced with such a pronounced drop, it is logical to ask if there are specific factors that triggered the sales on XRP. The answer is affirmative because behind the collapse of XRP quotes there is the decision of the American SEC to sue Ripple. According to the U.S. market regulator, Ripple company would have violated the laws of the States that regulate the sale of unregistered securities. As soon as the news spread, Ripple's CEO Brad Garlinghouse immediately took a position stating that the lawsuit that has been filed by the SEC is "fundamentally wrong as a matter of fact and law".

17. Uniswap The Pink Unicorn

Uniswap is a set of computer programs running on the Ethereum blockchain that enable decentralized token swaps. The system works with the help of a few unicorns (as they illustrate in the logo).

Traders can swap Ethereum tokens on Uniswap without having to entrust their funds to anyone. In addition, anyone can lend their crypto to special reserves called liquidity pools, receiving commissions as a reward for the money provided.

Uniswap started out as a project designed to offer two functions: first, to serve as a DEX, in other words, a decentralized exchange within the Ethereum ecosystem. Second, to serve as an automated liquidity protocol (automated market maker or AMM).

The fact that Uniswap relies on Ethereum and its smart contacts to achieve this goal ensures that no centralization is required for its operation.

In concrete terms, Uniswap is a completely autonomous system that follows only one thing: its own programming, which is transparent and immutable.

The beginnings of the project are quite unique because it all started with a series of posts created by Vitalik Buteri, the founder of Ethereum in 2017, where Buterin had envisioned the possibility of creating DEX on Ethereum.

For years, centralized exchanges have been the backbone of the cryptocurrency market. They offer fast settlement times, high trading volume, and ever-improving liquidity. However, there is a parallel world built in the form of trustless protocols. Decentralized exchanges (DEX) do not require any intermediary or custodian to facilitate trading.

Due to the inherent limitations of blockchain technology, it has been difficult to create DEXs that can truly compete with their centralized counterparts. Much of DEX needs improvement in both performance and user experience.

The goal of the project seems to be clear: to create large pools of cryptocurrencies ready to be traded and, as a result, generate profits for the liquidity providers and the platform itself.

Without having to get too technical about the functionality of the coin, as it is overly complex and difficult, especially for those who are new to the cryptocurrency market, I summarize below in brief what are the advantages and disadvantages of the Uniswap cryptocurrency.

The **Advantages** are definitely these:

1.   It is a completely decentralized system.

2.   The protocol can be accessed using any web3 wallet (MetaMask) and create custom applications on them.

3.   Ability to create an exchange for any ERC-20 token.

4.   It is a non-profit project and completely open source.

5.   Trading within the platform is inexpensive.

6.   Liquidity pools offer good levels of profit for their providers.

The **Disadvantages** might be these instead:

1.   Gas usage from the platform is high. Given Ethereum's current scalability issues, the fees for the system and its operations on the blockchain turn out to be quite expensive.

2.   Uniswap is highly experimental like almost all current DeFi technologies. Because of this, you need to be aware that everything can go wrong, very wrong with the risk of losing your money if you do not know what you are doing.

18. Enjin Coin: The Cryptocurrency Linked to Gaming

Enjin coin (abbreviated ENJ) is a cryptocurrency created by the Enjin company for buying and selling virtual assets in the gaming industry. Enjin Coin was born as a response to the problem of the numerous frauds/scams that occur when it comes to buying and selling video game assets, to the point of evolving into a sort of "Ethereum for video games".

Since its creation in 2009, Enjin has become one of the largest online game community creation platforms, providing users with tools to create community, clan, and guild websites. A guild, for those who are not gaming experts, is a group of players who share the same purpose. In general, a guild is created to bring together a large number of people who are looking to move up in the rankings, organize tournaments between friends, trade cards, share techniques.

For the unfamiliar, virtual items are digital representations of functional or decorative items, such as clothing, weapons, or equipment, that players can purchase and use in the game environment to enhance their experience as players.

This makes it difficult for players to trade digital assets outside of the game environment or across platforms. Enjin Coin seeks to change that system. How does it do this? Simple. By using Enjin Coins as a common currency, games and communities can create unique in-game items, currencies, and privilege tokens, allowing players to trade digital items between different games. This changes the current virtual goods market from a centralized one to a decentralized one, encouraging players, game publishers, and content creators to trade, create, and manage virtual goods that should help Enjin quite a bit in the virtual goods markets, potentially increasing the value of the currency.

Just to give some numbers, it has been estimated that in 2020 only, the market for gaming-related virtual goods will be around USD 17 Billion.

The two co-founders of Enjin are Maxim Blagov and Witek Radomski. Maxim is a visionary and creative director with 18 years of experience in creative direction, project management and UX design. He is an expert in developing concepts and strategies for large interactive applications. Witek has overseen Enjin's technical engineering for nearly a decade.

The two founders decided to take the first steps of the virtuate currency with a very smart move: given the high number of "Minecraft" players, who are used to use Enjin, they chose Minecraft as the first test to launch the virtual currency. With time, this new virtual currency has become stronger and stronger, acquiring more and more concreteness and confidence in gamers and also in various international investors.

In 2019, Enjin, following its partnership with Samsung and Unity, had its token increase in value by approximately 500% in the next 90 days following the news. On January 19, 2020, Enjin Coin (ENJ) became the first gaming-related crypto to receive the green light from the Japanese Virtual Currency Exchange Association, the JVCEA. This coincided with a sudden 71% increase in the coin's dollar value, which occurred in just 9 hours: the price of ENJ went from USD 0.236340 to a peak of USD 0.406356. After entering the Japanese country, CEO Blagov stated, "From Super Mario to Pokémon and Final Fantasy, Japan is home to pioneering video games that hold an enduring place in pop culture. Japan's culture of innovation is aligned with Enjin's. We believe that some of the world's best blockchain titles will come from the Japanese industry, and we will be there to help them make the most of this powerful technology."

Enjin's strategy for success is pretty clear: the more developers adopt Enjin's coin features, the more players will use the Enjoin coin, which will create network and network and increasingly strengthen the coin.

In 2021, the coin has a market price of about 0.565275 USD.

What forecast can this cryptocurrency have in the future?

Definitely positive and of growth.

The problem of the lack of transparency of the assets that still exist on the most popular video games, is a huge problem and Enjin has the solution to solve it. Enjin has as a solid base a community of millions of players and 250.000 communities, but the interest in cryptomoneta is extending more and more also to investors, who do not attend the world of gaming, but who really believe in the development of this virtual currency doing their best to make it happen.

The partnerships with Samsung and Unity are the two biggest partnerships the cryptocurrency world has seen so far, and Enjin is also widely supported and appreciated by the CEOs of Binance and Ethereum. There are no competitors currently in this industry, there are competitors in gaming but not in tokenizing assets. Enjin is part together with BAT and DENT of the only three tokens to have exceeded 10 million users.

19. Miner and Mining to Earn Cryptocurrencies

Mining is the operation that is done in cryptocurrencies in general, to issue/discover new currency and get it into circulation in the market.

As with miners who bring up gold through mining, a similar process takes place for bitcoins, but in a digital version.

The blockchain stores each transaction within data structures called blocks, as mentioned earlier. Thanks to mining, you can add new blocks to the Blockchain, said in simple words mining is nothing more than the processing to find an exact code very complex to find, with a succession of attempts, by a computer processor that can be the Cpu of a computer, the Gpu of a graphics card, ASICs and other hardware systems.

Whoever finds such a code is rewarded, in the case of bitcoin, with an amount of 12.5 bitcoins (an amount that will decrease over time), plus all the transaction fees he put in the block as an incentive for the mining time used.

Those who perform this operation are called Miners.

Everyone can become a "Miner" and start trying to solve the complex mathematical problem related to new blocks, so that this is created in a valid and cryptographic way and can be added to the Blockchain.

Be aware that, however, as time goes by it is increasingly difficult to mine as the number of Bitcoins totally available is defined and not unlimited (21 Million).

20. Pi Network: An Exceptional New Way of Conceiving Cryptocurrencies, or a Big Fake?

Pi Network can be considered a revolutionary cryptocurrency that anyone can create (or "mine") through an app installed on a smartphone device, all without consuming battery or data traffic beyond the normal use of the phone.

Pi Network's mining takes place entirely on the user's smartphone, via the project's official App: all you have to do is confirm the mining activity on a daily basis (in essence, put a click) to receive a small number of tokens. Each miner also, through an invitation from their smartphone can invite other people to download the app, helping to mine. It works as a kind of affiliate marketing, where people who mine are traceable to the person who sent the invitation.

For this reason, each individual, as within a pyramid system, earns a higher percentage of Pi, thanks also to the contribution of other miners. That is why it becomes especially important to spam one's own affiliate code as much as possible in order to generate more Pi Network income.

Today there are more than 13 million miners worldwide, who support the system through their devices.

At the beginning of 2021 it is impossible to buy Pi Network on any exchange.

Nowadays it is not possible to understand if this will remain just a prestigious project of three Stanford students founded in 2018, or if it will be able to make a real up grade and become for all intents and purposes a real cryptocurrency that can be bought, sold, and exchanged like other established virtual currencies. The fact remains, however, that to date this coin continues to gain acceptance, significantly increasing the number of its miners.

The founders, who often appear on the app with short messages, have stated that by the end of 2021 PI should become a real currency.

We will see. To date, my advice, since it costs nothing, is to download the app and simply click the button a couple of times a day to "mine" and involve and share the project with as many friends and acquaintances as possible, so that by mining under you increase your percentage of PI. In the worst-case scenario, you will have lost a couple of minutes of your twenty-four hours a daytime, nothing compared to what normal people spend unnecessarily on social networks in a totally unproductive way, but the FOMO (Fear Of Missing Out) is a lot, that is to have missed an experimental project that may or may not be (this we will see only with the passage of time) the revolution, as were the Bitcoins in 2009.

Who would have bet on Bitcoins in 2009?

Everyone, even big investors, and industry gurus, distanced themselves from it. Many considered it crazy. No one wanted them for a few cents of dollars, and yet, today everyone is vying, Banks, Investment Funds, Billionaires, and private citizens to buy a virtual currency that has touched $50,000 USD in value every single coin. Since the speculative bubble of the new economy, much has changed. People work from home in Smart working, they receive food at home through deliveries, we go around with bicycles rented on the street and in a while, we are going to vacation on Mars!

I am not saying it is a winning choice without a shadow of a doubt, maybe it will not go extremely far, but it is always better to be up to date on what is around us.

As Charles Darwin would say: "it is not the strongest or the most intelligent species that survives, but the one that adapts best to change".

21. What is Matic Network?

Matic Network is a blockchain platform that aims to increase the scalability of Ethereum by speeding up transactions and making them cheaper.

This ambitious goal can be achieved, according to Matic Network's developers, by implementing secondary blockchains to handle transactions faster.

Matic Network's innovative architecture takes advantage of Ethereum's Plasma feature to integrate the different blockchains, leaving the main one with the task of periodically verifying the legitimacy of transactions.

An epoch-making change that would allow a Matic sidechain to process up to 2 16 transactions per block, a goal that still seems far away for the majority of blockchains.

Transactions that occur on Matic Network are validated through a proof of stake algorithm, thus giving individual users the ability to network their funds and receive a reward for maintaining the network.

Having almost instantaneous transactions would allow Ethereum to further increase its market share in the field of decentralized applications.

But in the future of Matic Network there does not seem to be only Ethereum, because the developers have stated that they are already working to implement their solution on the Bitcoin blockchain as well.

Matic Network's development team is based in India, although it can boast of collaborators all over the world.

On April 24, 2019 Matic Network carried out its IEO (Initial Exchange Offering) on Binance Launchpad, where 19% of the total token offering was sold at a unit price of USD 0.003, raising over USD 5 Million.

On April 29, it was officially announced on Matic's blog the participation in the funding round by Coinbase to support the Matic Network project.

22. Facebook and Cryptocurrencies: The Libra Project and the Switch to Diem Coin

Even the giant Facebook has shown itself to be seriously interested in Cryptocurrencies. Zuckerberg's company had launched Libra, a project that seemed remarkably interesting, focusing on the consolidated base of users already enrolled in Facebook (about 2 billion) and Instagram (about 1 billion) around the world. Unfortunately, the launch of their virtual currency got off to a disastrous start.

After the scandal emerged of Cambridge Analytica, a political data analytics company that used the personal information of more than 50 million Facebook users, issues related to privacy and the use of sensitive data were for Zuckerberg's company, no small problem, which brought an initial loss of trust and credibility. Millions of users abandoned the platform, and the market capitalization had suffered a sharp decline, from 538 to 464 billion dollars. As you can imagine, regrettably, this situation of uncertainty has had strong repercussions on the Libra project; after the mistrust and the negative trend that was created around Facebook important partners such as PayPal, Visa and Mastercard have decided to discontinue their partnership with Libra, cracking in a serious way its launch.

To date Facebook is working to resolve all the issues of the passing, making a serious effort to regain the trust of users, implementing concrete and serious projects to protect the privacy of its users. Also, the cryptocurrency project has been resumed, reformulated and concretely reshaped.

The first act of re-launch was the change of name, to mark a real clean break with the past.

The cryptocurrency Libra has taken on a new name: Diem Coin, in an effort to demonstrate that the project has "organizational independence" as it attempts to gain regulatory approvals to launch.

It looks like Facebook is getting more serious about blockchain, having recently appointed a chief technology officer dedicated to the technology.

The social media giant named one of its senior engineers, Evan Cheng, as its first "Director of Blockchain Engineering."

According to the Financial Times, cryptocurrency could debut as a single currency backed by the U.S. dollar, with an initial launch already set for the first half of 2021.

The Diem project aims to provide a simple and usable platform for fintech innovation to enable consumers and businesses to conduct instant, secure, and low-cost transactions.

Mark Zuckerberg, in a post on Facebook wrote about cryptocurrencies:

"For example, one of the most interesting questions in technology right now is about centralization versus decentralization. Many of us are converging on this technology because we believe it can be a decentralizing force that puts more power in people's hands.

In the 1990s and 2000s, most people believed that technology would be a decentralizing force. But today, many people have lost faith in that promise. With the rise of a small number of large technology companies - and governments using technology to watch their citizens - many people now believe that technology centralizes power instead of decentralizing it.

There are important countertrends to this - like cryptocurrencies - that take power away from centralized systems and put it back into the hands of people. But they come with the risk of being harder to control. I am interested in learning more and studying the ins and outs of these technologies and how best to use them in our services.

This will be a serious year of self-improvement, and I look forward to learning from the work to solve our problems together."

How will Facebook Coin Diem Dollar work?

Users will have to register to use the coin, but Facebook will guarantee that wallets and transactions will be completely anonymous.

There are rumors in the financial circles that the coin will be launched on the Ethereum blockchain.

Given Facebook's massive size and reach, it seems safe to assume that the ICO can compete with the $1.2 billion that Telegram raised in its own funding round.

The listing and price of Diem Dollar is expected to be extremely high and, as we said, it will probably be a stable coin so no price fluctuations and it will be tied to the US dollar.

Mark Zuckerberg strongly wants Facebook's Diem to become a really effective digital currency that can be spent by users every day.

With much interest and curiosity, we will follow the progress and developments of this new project.

23. Major Investors in Cryptocurrencies and New Billionaires

Elon Musk, a great character of which we have already spoken in previous pages, is to date one of the most esteemed and eclectic billionaires on the planet. Musk announced in early 2021 that through his company "Tesla", manufacturer of electric vehicles and more, has informed the SEC, the authority that oversees the markets in the U.S., to have invested the equivalent of $ 1.5 billion in Bitcoin. His decision has created quite a stir towards this digital currency, and it is assumed that many other major investors will follow the path marked by Elon. The same Musk has also announced that in the short term it will also be possible to buy his cars directly with Bitcoins.

There are many who know **the Winklevoss twins**, those who at the time invested in cryptocurrencies, then still semi unknown, the compensation obtained in court by Mark Zuckerberg. The two brothers had invented a social network reserved for Harvard university students, called Harvardconnection.com. They called Zuckerberg to develop the idea, but after a few months, the latter withdrew from the project.

After the birth of Facebook, the Winklevoss brothers sued Facebook for theft of intellectual property, with a claim for damages of USD 600 Million. The parties reached a settlement of USD 65 million.

The twins invested part of the settlement, about USD 11 Million by buying Bitcoins when their value was USD 120. To date, necessary calculator in hand, their personal wealth in cryptocurrency is expected to be around USD 1.4 Billion. Not bad!

We have previously mentioned the mysterious **Satoshi Nakamoto**, the inventor of Bitcoin, who kept for himself a million pieces, parked in a wallet never touched: at today's values, they are over 35 billion dollars, which makes Satoshi the billionaire in 35th place in Bloomberg's ranking.

Vitalik Buterin, born in 1994, is a writer and programmer born in Russia and raised in Canada, endowed from an early age with an innate intelligence and a vivid interest in technology. Since 2011, he has been involved as a journalist and co-founder of Bitcoin Magazine. Vitalik is a true "Rockstar" in the cryptocurrency world, despite his simplicity and shyness. He gets invited to conventions, signs autograph, lends himself to taking photos. All this popularity is linked to the fact that he is no less than the inventor of Ethereum, the second most popular cryptocurrency after Bitcoin.

Today, Buterin owns 330,000 Ethereum. Given the current market value of 18,000 U.S. dollars, his assets in euros should be around 594 Million USD.

Among other superfans, financial wizards and cryptocurrency investors, one cannot fail to mention entrepreneur and venture capitalist **Matthew Roszak**, with an estimated wealth of around USD 1.2 Billion.

He is followed closely by entrepreneur **Tim Draper**, with assets of around USD 1.1 Billion.

In the ranking we also find **Micheal Saylor** with a capital of about 600 million and finally **Mike Novogratz**, with about 478 million USD.

It only remains for me to hope that in a few years, or in the next decade, we can also include **Your Name** in a chapter like this, my dear reader.

I wish you nothing but the best in this business, where the best, well, is the absolute best that one could dream of.

24. What are the Market Trends regarding Cryptocurrencies?

What is halving? It is an "event" that occurs every 4 years and results in the halving of the amount of cryptocurrency produced.

So today the amount issued every 10 minutes has dropped from 12.5 to 6.25. During the previous two halving, in 2016 and 2012, Bitcoin was responsible for a growth in the following 18 months of about 9,000 percent. And if it goes the same way this time around, we could end up with Bitcoin at USD 300,000 by December 2021.

Even the giant Jp Morgan, which has always rowed against Bitcoin, has now changed its mind, reporting how several family offices and large investors are approaching cryptocurrency. According to Jp Morgan, in a scenario where all pension funds and insurance companies in the U.S., U.K., Eurozone and Japan invested 1% of their assets in Bitcoin, it would create an additional demand for the most emblazoned of cryptocurrencies of USD 600 billion, roughly double its current capitalization.

The investment bank Morgan Stanley, through its Counterpoint Global investment unit that manages USD 150 billion in assets, is planning to raise many Bitcoins in the market, thus unveiling its bullish bias on the cryptocurrency.

This prediction has also been confirmed by Social Capital analyst Chamat Palihapitya, who says, "*Bitcoin will probably rise to USD 100K, then USD 150K, then USD 200K.*" However, the timing remains uncertain, which could correspond to 5, or maybe 10 years. Regardless, experts are almost convinced that it will reach those figures.

Deutsche Bank is set to provide a new custody service for large financial institutions that are planning to invest in cryptocurrencies, according to analysts. The project, called Deutsche Bank Digital Asset Custody, will be able to open up the world of crypto for the German bank's clients.

25. The Main Scams Related to Cryptocurrencies

In the world of the web in general and in particular that of cryptocurrencies it is very important to protect yourself and, as I have already pointed out several times before, to raise your security levels because scams are extremely widespread, and you must always secure yourself and your investments.

1. Automated Trading Systems.

Let us start with the most notorious Cryptocurrency scam, which is related to Automated Trading Systems.

Such scam traders have the sole interest in getting you to pour your capital into the coffers of an unregulated broker, usually on offshore territories, where your money becomes unrecoverable. Their only goal is to take a percentage of your deposited capital.

2. Malware.

Fraudsters who carry out this kind of fraud do not steal credit card information or bank account details but develop "crypto-malware" that is produced to enter your wallet and steal your funds. Therefore, as already mentioned in the security chapter, it is particularly important to protect your personal electronic device with antivirus and anti-malware. Among the most used malicious viruses is "Coinhive" which is designed to design the cryptocurrency Monero when a user visits a web page, without his approval. Just to give you an idea, this type of malware in 2017 alone had already infected 12% of companies globally.

3. Phishing.

Generally, these people receive an email that looks like the one you usually receive from the bank you are using. Usually, the messages include a link that directs you to a platform that looks like the one you are actually using but is actually hiding an actual scam. Once you provide the personal information or data that the scammer will ask you to enter, he will have all the necessary details to access your account.

4. ICO Scams.

An ICO is an Initial Coin Offer. That is, an initial offer of a new currency. Thanks to cryptocurrencies, in fact, anyone can issue their own currency. Only that usually a newly issued currency, has no great value. However, if you were able to buy a coin when it has just been issued and therefore having truly little value, if it were to increase in value you could earn a lot without doing anything. Obviously, cyber criminals on the Net have spread a lot of totally fake and fraudulent ICO offers. For this reason, it is advisable not to make any purchase if: there is no accurate or updated information of the company that generated the coin, we do not find any news on the Net about the company that issues the coin and if we notice questionable business practices, such as insider trading.

5. DAO theft.

On the net some DAO (decentralized autonomous organizations) have successfully issued their own crypto currencies. These systems can be an exceptionally good earning system, especially if at the beginning we have little money to invest and can't afford a too famous virtual currency. Unfortunately, however, these systems are less secure. In 2016, for example, a DAO system was tampered with by a hacker who stole a third of the group's total coins on their account.

6. Abusive Cryptomining.

In the world one in five companies is affected by hacker attacks that exploit the computing power of unsuspecting users' personal computers to generate cryptocurrency, using other people's energy and facilities. In order to mine and earn cryptocurrency, it is necessary to use computers that are powerful in terms of both core and graphics card structure, operating 24 hours a day seven days a week. A side aspect of mining, in fact, is that it consumes a lot of electricity (think of having many computers on 365 days a year in perpetual operation).

So, what did the Hackers think?

They thoughts: why can't I exploit other people's computers to save energy and use the power of unsuspecting citizens' computers for free to make money?

A curious episode related to the possibility of undermining "exploiting" the facilities of others is that of some Russian scientists who were arrested. For what reason? Well, the latter have thought well, working in the nuclear research center (VNIEF) of Sarov, 229 miles from Moscow, to generate cryptocurrencies by exploiting the supercomputer of the research center. Obviously, to make a real, substantial profit from mining requires computing power, cheap electricity, and dedicated infrastructure.

I was surprised, several years ago, to discover that in a small state like Iceland, a place renowned for its unspoiled nature, its expanses, whale watching, let us say for attracting a certain kind of tourism was actually an ideal place for cryptocurrency mining. A decisive factor for the profitable mining and miner business is access to cheap energy. Iceland's geothermal power plants along with low temperatures for cooling data centers make the country one of the world's leading cryptocurrency mining locations. I was quite impressed to see these huge Hangars full of servers and endless data centers, super supervised, not far from the capital Reykjavik, creating a certain contrast, between the almost fairy-tale and retro landscape of the city and this hyper technological world with the contours not yet clear for most of the world population.

Summary:

1. Automated Trading Systems.

2. Malware.

3. Phishing.

4. ICO Scams.

5. DAO theft.

6. Abusive Crypto mining.

26. How the New HashGraph Technology Works

More and more often, you hear people in the industry talking about Hashgraph.

However, what is it really about?

Basically, it is nothing but a new technology that would replace the most famous and well-known Blockchain.

A blockchain is a distributed database (Distributed Ledger Technology, DLT) whose state evolves over time. A classic example of a state is a ledger with account balances, but in reality, it can be anything: for example, in Ethereum, it is the state of the EVM contains all the states of all the smart contracts in the network. It is difficult, though, to define a global state for a distributed system: each node participating in the network has its own local state, so there are actually as many versions of the state as the number of nodes in the network. A huge number! To define the global state of the blockchain, you need an efficient protocol that allows all participating nodes to agree on the same state and update their local states accordingly.

Proof of Work, still used by several major blockchains such as Bitcoin and Ethereum, was created to prevent a malicious actor from creating a multitude of fake nodes with which to approve a state, an attack known as a Sybil Attack.

Blockchains are organized into chains of blocks approved by the network when proposed along with the proof of work (the "nonce") performed by the node that produced the block. To find this "nonce" special equipment (GPUs and ASICs) and an amount of electricity are used; a transaction to be finalized must wait to be included in a block, and then confirmed by an indefinite number of blocks in order to avoid possible reorganization of the chain (danger of double spending).

As the years go by, it is becoming more and more evident what the limitations of blockchain are: the distributed, anonymous, and encrypted ledger that is the basis of Bitcoin and Ethereum smart contracts. The first problem encountered by this technology concerns its slowness: today, the blockchain can validate no more than 7 transactions per second, thus placing a major limitation on its diffusion (to make a comparison, a circuit like Visa is able to handle 60 thousand transactions per second).

The second problem even takes the form of a dilemma: to increase the number of transactions validated every second, it would be sufficient to increase the size of the blocks that contain the encrypted information; but increasing their size has as a consequence that fewer and fewer nodes (the users who have downloaded the ledger on their computers) will have the computational power necessary to "mine" on the blockchain, thus decreasing the decentralization that is one of the aspects that guarantees its security (to date, for example, 11 thousand nodes are active in the Bitcoin ledger).

The third issue concerns energy consumption: analyst Alex de Vries has estimated that a single Bitcoin deposit requires the amount of energy needed to maintain a home for a week. Not only that: according to other calculations, the energy needed every hour to mine bitcoin is equivalent to the annual energy needs of a country like Ecuador. It is clear that such energy consumption cannot be sustainable in the long term, not least because it is bound to increase more and more (but some possible solutions are beginning to appear).

It is for all these reasons that a scientific paper - recently presented by the software house Swirlds - has attracted a lot of attention. It introduces the technology that, according to its creators, should make the blockchain obsolete: Hashgraph, a distributed ledger characterized by higher speed (up to 300 thousand transactions per second), higher security and lower energy consumption.

What if we imagine a distributed ledger that goes beyond blocks, Proof of Work, and Proof of Stake? A system where transactions no longer have to wait for a block to be finalized to be approved by the network, and where an inordinate amount of energy is not used to solve mathematical problems for their own sake?

Hedera Hashgraph was born in 2015 from an idea of Leemon Baird, co-founder and CTO of Swirlds, a New York-based software company, and aims to be:

- A cryptocurrency (HBAR) with native support for micro-transactions.

- A distributed file storage system.

- A platform for smart contracts written in Solidity.

Surely thinking about a new technology, given the consolidation of the business of virtual currencies, given the increasing number of operations and transactions is definitely a step that must be taken to improve the system and the world of cryptocurrency and first of all to try to limit consumption, to make it super-fast and to protect our environment.

27. Cryptocurrencies, Dark Web and Silk Road

Thanks to cryptocurrencies, black markets are experiencing a sort of "renaissance". The ability to transfer money anonymously and the very idea of a decentralized currency have greatly reduced the possibilities of transaction control by governments, states, and special services such as espionage.

The most emblematic story of an online black market is that of Silk Road, a topic known to all those who have been dealing with cryptocurrencies for a long time. The main feature of the site was the use of Bitcoin and the possibility to pay for purchases through the anonymous network Tor.

Silk Road gained popularity due to the opportunity to purchase the various prohibited drugs and other substances, pirated software, stolen goods, and a huge number of other illegal goods.

Despite the anonymity, US intelligence services invested heavily in shutting down the black market and after nearly two years of investigation, in October 2013, Silk Road owner and administrator William Ross Ulbricht was arrested. After him, several of his employees and dealers also went down with him.

Despite selling prohibited merchandise, the creator of Silk Road adhered to an extremely strict code of ethics. In particular, he prohibited the sale of weapons and the services of murderers. But this did not help him avoid punishment: for his crimes, he received two life sentences in the United States.

The first platform, after the famous "Silk Road", was the Silk Road 2.0 marketplace. However, Silk Road 2.0 also turned out to be an intelligence trap. One of the confidants of Blake Benthall, the founder of the said black market, who worked with him from the beginning turned out to be an FBI agent. The main goal of the feds was to capture the major dealers who remained at large after Silk Road 1.0 and it was achieved.

One more successor to Silk Road was the **"Evolution"** black market. However, this platform did not last long and in March 2015 the founder of Evolution suddenly disappeared into thin air taking about USD 12 million with him.

It should be noted, that of all the black markets in the Darknet, it was Evolution that enjoyed the reputation of a reliable marketplace. On Evolution, a three-confirmation signature was used for every payment: the transaction had to be confirmed by both the buyer and the retailer, as well as the platform administration.

Another "key feature" of the Evolution platform was the complete lack of regulation of the services offered, in simple terms you could sell and buy almost anything: fake documents, drugs, weapons, etc.

Another immensely popular black market, but currently closed, was **"Sheep Marketplace"**. As for the closure, it is said on the web that this happened due to a hack, which is very unlikely, since the withdrawal of funds from the platform was stopped a week before the site went offline. The amount stolen is also impressive: over 150,000 BTC for a total of about USD 40 million.

At the moment, with the beginnings of 2021, black market activity in the deep web has all but ceased despite the harsh crackdown and scams that have characterized the industry, in fact, many online black markets are active, including Empire Market, Icarus Market and Bitbazaar Market.

28. Cryptocurrencies and The Environment: Pollution-Related Side Effects

Although perhaps no one thinks about connecting the two, one downside, unfortunately, of cryptocurrencies is global pollution. It is a factor that is often not thought of, since the topic at hand is about virtual currencies, and yet, it is.

The Bitcoin network alone in the world is responsible for an amount of CO_2 emissions of over 22 million tons per year.

Statistics in hand, BTC cause the emission of CO_2 equal to those produced in a year by the City of Las Vegas, or the entire Sri Lanka.

How is all this possible?

The answer is quite simple: to generate and validate a transaction in Bitcoin requires solving a complex mathematical puzzle using a computational system.

This process requires an enormous amount of energy.

Most of the miners, which as specified above are the "verifiers" of Bitcoin transitions, are concentrated 68% in Asia, 15% in North America and 17% in Europe.

The research was carried out by researchers at the Technical University of Munich.

If on the one hand the process is unstoppable and mining operations are essential to maintain the system, what could be possible solutions to reduce the environmental impact?

One solution could be, in order to improve the ecological balance of the ecosystem, to connect more and more networks of miners to sources of renewable generation, giving more support and push to green energies. It is hoped that there will be a greater level of attention from this point of view to ensure a better world for future generations.

Final Considerations

I would like to conclude the book with some of my personal considerations and thank you for the preference given to me by reading up to this last chapter.

So, since cryptocurrencies are practically universally recognized currencies now, they can be used all over the world, and with a large type and variety of users, without any problems.

One of the reasons why investing in cryptocurrencies can be really advantageous nowadays is also constituted by the processing costs: these, for each operation, are very reduced, unlike what happens for other types of currency, which imply much higher rates and management costs.

Personally, I think that it is worth investing in cryptocurrencies because they are the instrument of the moment; because they are going through an exponential growth; because they could continue this trend, also considering their nature of being born limited, to have an end to their proliferation just to avoid inflation; and because on today's markets with the uncertainty that reigns supreme, paradoxically, just these virtual instruments would seem to be the most concrete.

Following the Pandemic caused by the Coronavirus that has affected the entire globe, many states have irreversibly started to print money. Well, maybe they printed too much money, and this could turn into inflation.

But one must ask: what exactly is inflation?

To such a question many are used to answer that it constitutes the increase in prices and decrease in purchasing power.

Just to give you an idea, The United States of America has printed more money in one month than in two centuries. Amazing, isn't it?

"The United States of America printed more money in June 2020 than in two centuries of history. Last month, the U.S. budget deficit of USD 864 billion was larger than the total debt accumulated between 1776 and 1979."

The Fed itself, using all the tools at its disposal to deal with the pandemic, including printing money, has kept interest rates close to zero and buying USD 120 billion worth of assets per month.

However, some analysts believe that inflation is indeed there, but that it is "hidden" in asset prices rather than consumer prices, given the role of money issuance in supporting the stock market during the pandemic.

Given the analysis I have just done, I think that humanity is undoubtedly at the beginning of a new era, a before and after pandemic, and for this reason I believe that the future is increasingly directed to virtual currencies and that over time they will be increasingly solid and consolidated.

Good luck and happy investing.

This has been:

The Beginner's Guide to Cryptocurrencies: What the New Rich Investor Teach Their Followers About Virtual Money

Five Parameters to Analyze, How to Create Your Asset and Choose the Best Currencies

www.ingramcontent.com/pod-product-compliance
Lightning Source LLC
Chambersburg PA
CBHW070401220526
45467CB00001B/448